Welcome to The Beginner Guitarist Book Four!

This book builds on the ideas and techniques explored in the first three books. It begins with an extensive look at A major, initially in second position but moving through other positions and finishing with an exercise in thirds and a duet.

The remainder focuses on triplets and compound time, beginning with triplet exercises in 2/4 before moving on to 6/8. The book then features swing rhythms before finishing with a Habanera, Renaissance pieces and a modern piece in multiple time signatures.

Published by
Chester Music Limited
14-15 Berners Street, London W1T 3LJ, UK.

Exclusive Distributors:
Music Sales Limited
Distribution Centre, Newmarket Road,
Bury St Edmunds, Suffolk IP33 3YB, UK.

Music Sales Pty Limited
20 Resolution Drive, Caringbah, NSW 2229, Australia.

Order No. CH79365
ISBN: 978-1-78038-490-0

This book © Copyright 2012 Chester Music Limited.

Unauthorised reproduction of any part of this publication by any means including photocopying is an infringement of copyright.

Written by Nigel Tuffs
Edited by Adrian Hopkins
Music processed by Paul Ewers Music Design
Design by Fresh Lemon
Printed in the EU

Chester Music part of The Music Sales Group
London / New York / Paris / Sydney / Copenhagen / Berlin / Madrid / Hong Kong / Tokyo

A Major (II Position)

Happy (Not Sad)

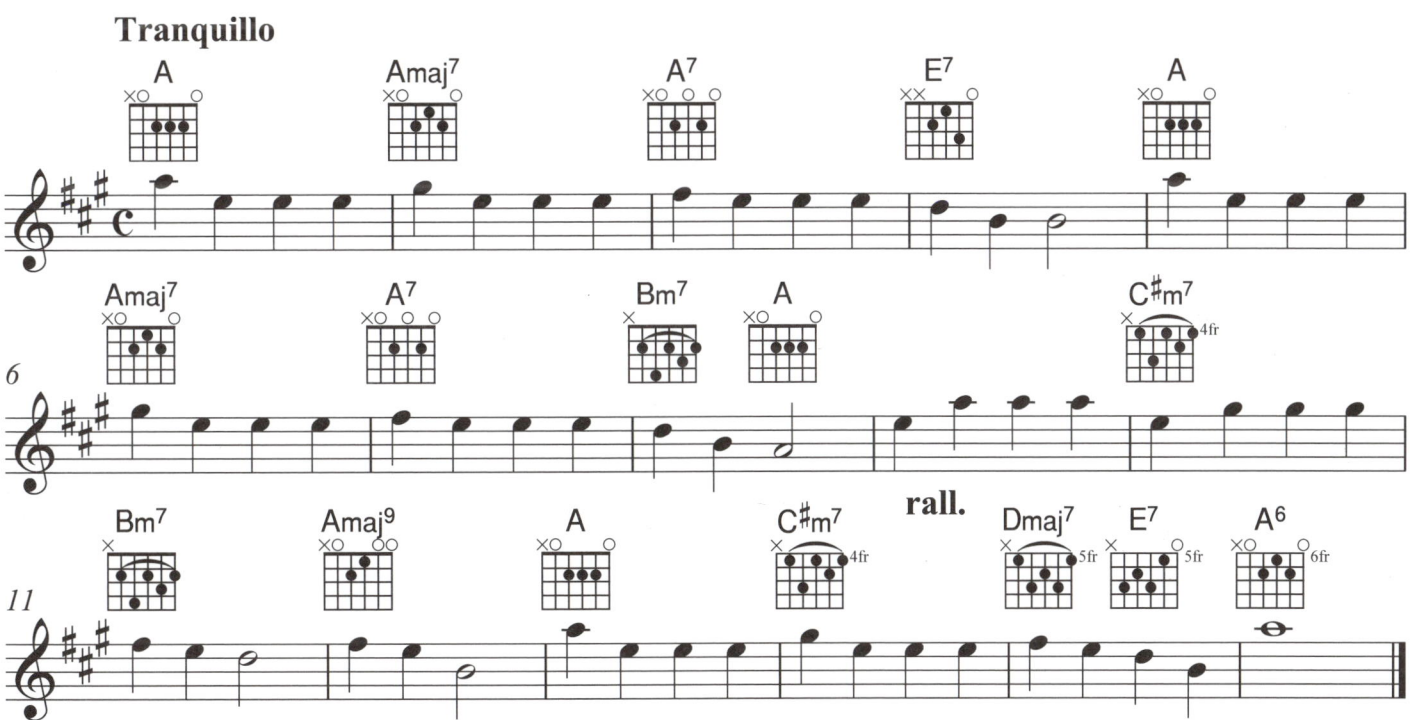

Allegretto in A

Matteo Carcassi (1792 – 1853)

TIP: Try playing the chords as a warm-up

Mrs. Winter's Jump

John Dowland (1563 – 1626)

Exercise in Thirds

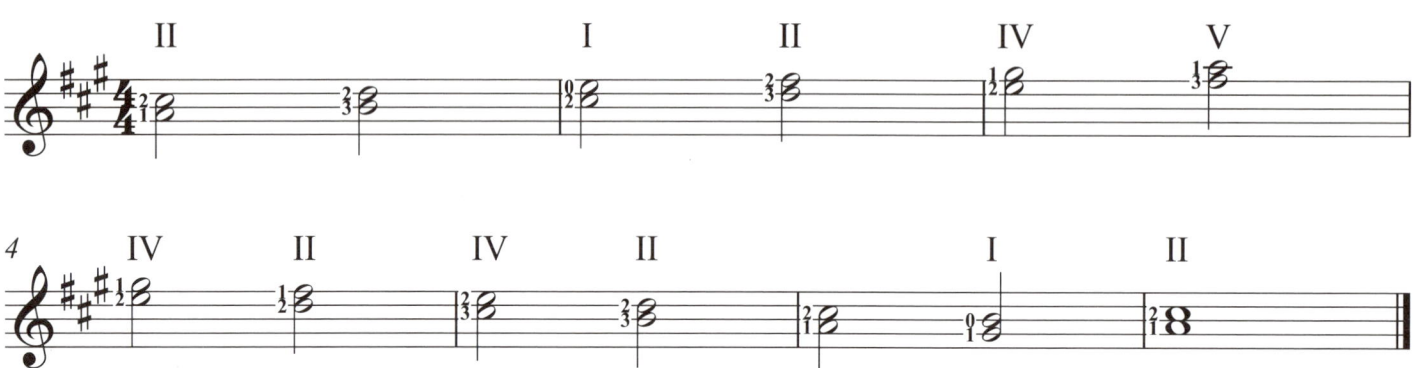

Rhythm Exercise

New Mexico

Bass Exercise

New Mexico Bass

TIP: Try playing as a duet with 'New Mexico'

Triplets and Compound Time

Exercise 1

Exercise 2

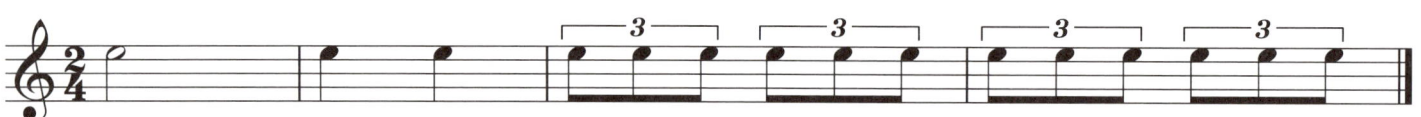

Exercise 3

Exercise 4

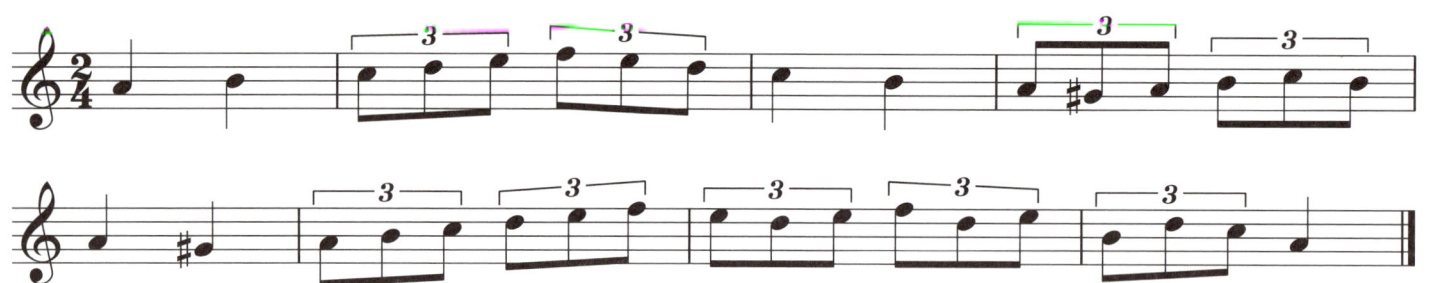

Gavotte

Johann Sebastian Bach (1685 – 1750)

TIP: Try playing without the bass line

Exercise 5

Exercise 6

Exercise 7

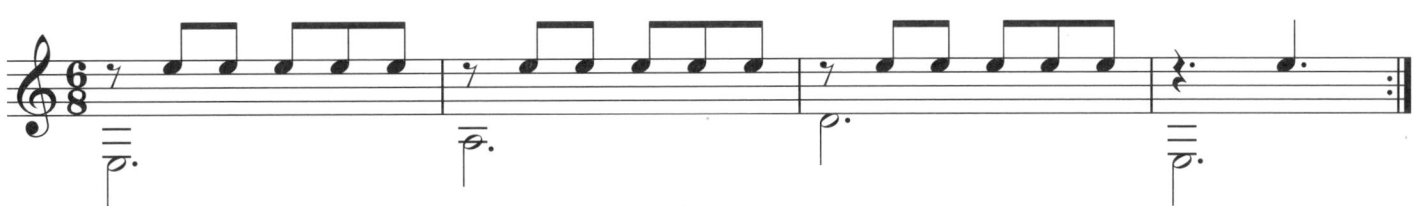

Etude in A Minor

Fernando Sor (1778 – 1839)

Semiquavers

Exercise 1

Exercise 2

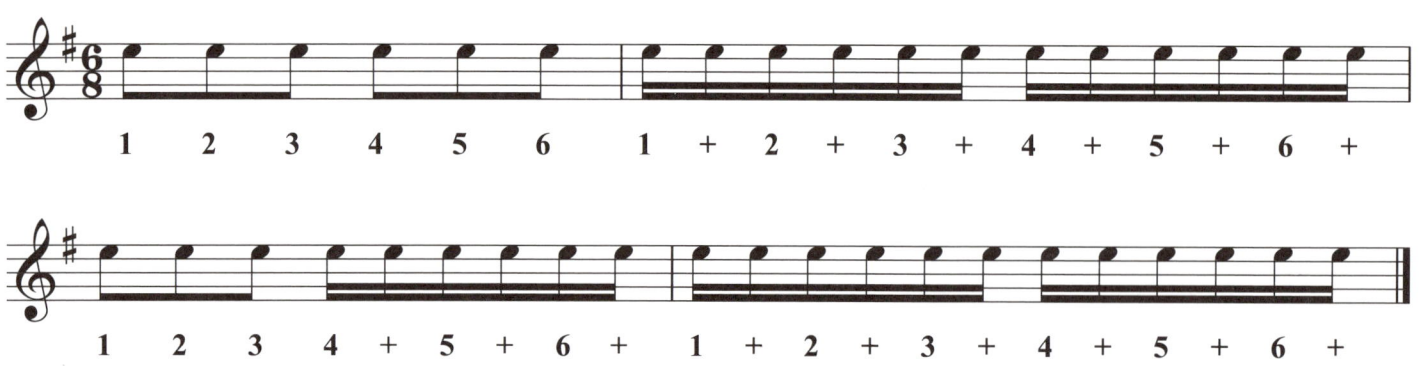

Exercise 3

E Natural Minor (VII Position)

Nocturne

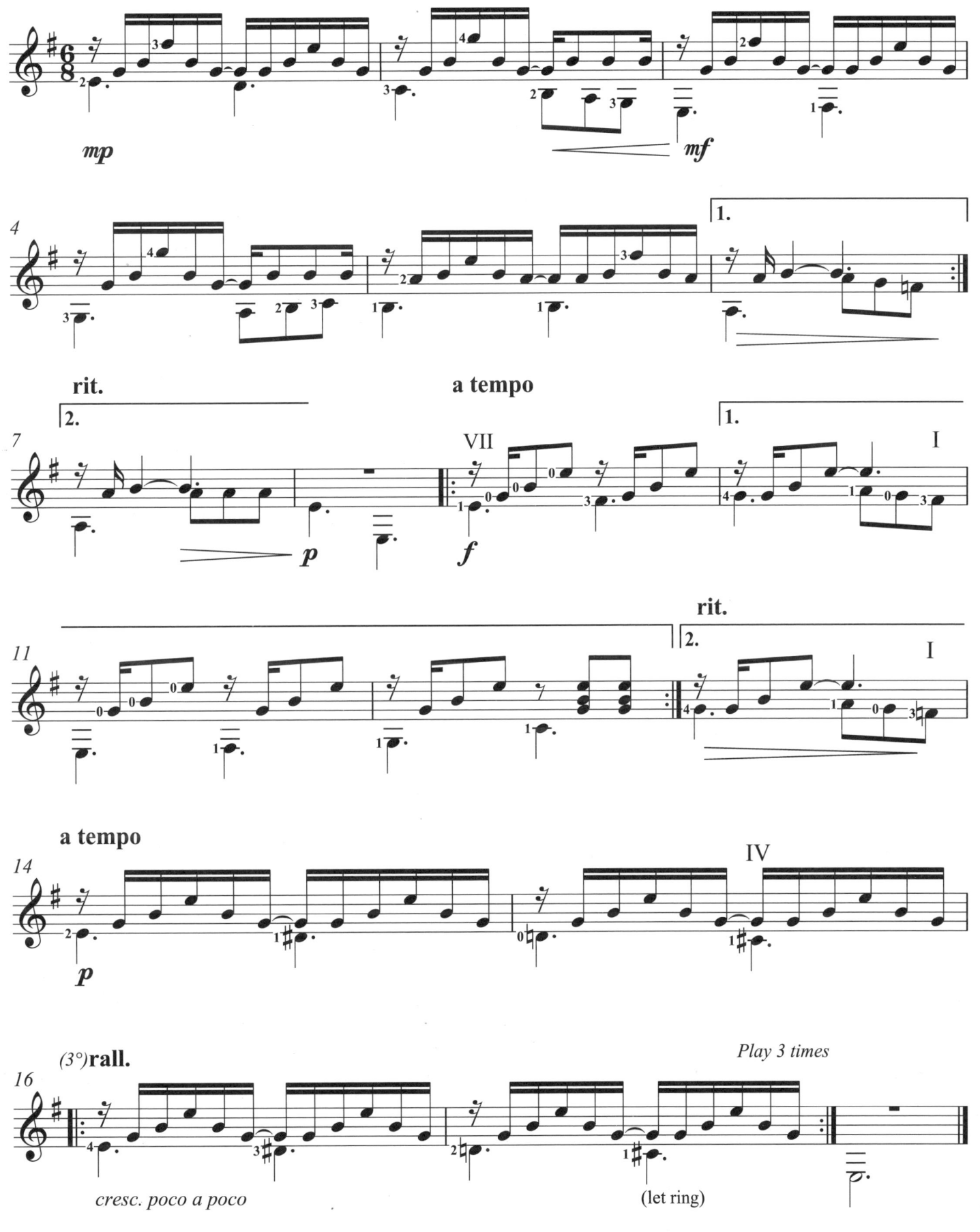

Triplets

Exercise 1

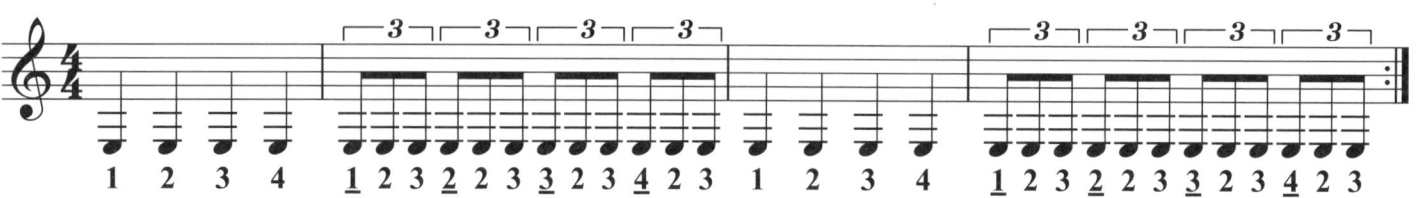

Exercise 2

Blues in E

D Blues Scale

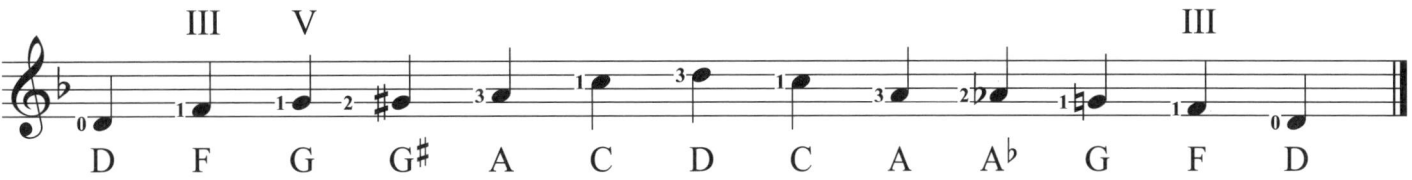

III V III
D F G G♯ A C D C A A♭ G F D

G Blues Scale

III V VI V III
G B♭ C C♯ D F G F D D♭ C B♭ G

D Blues

♩ = 100
1.
2.

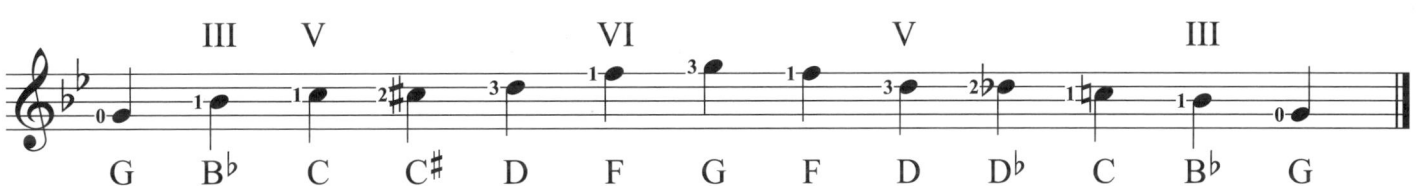

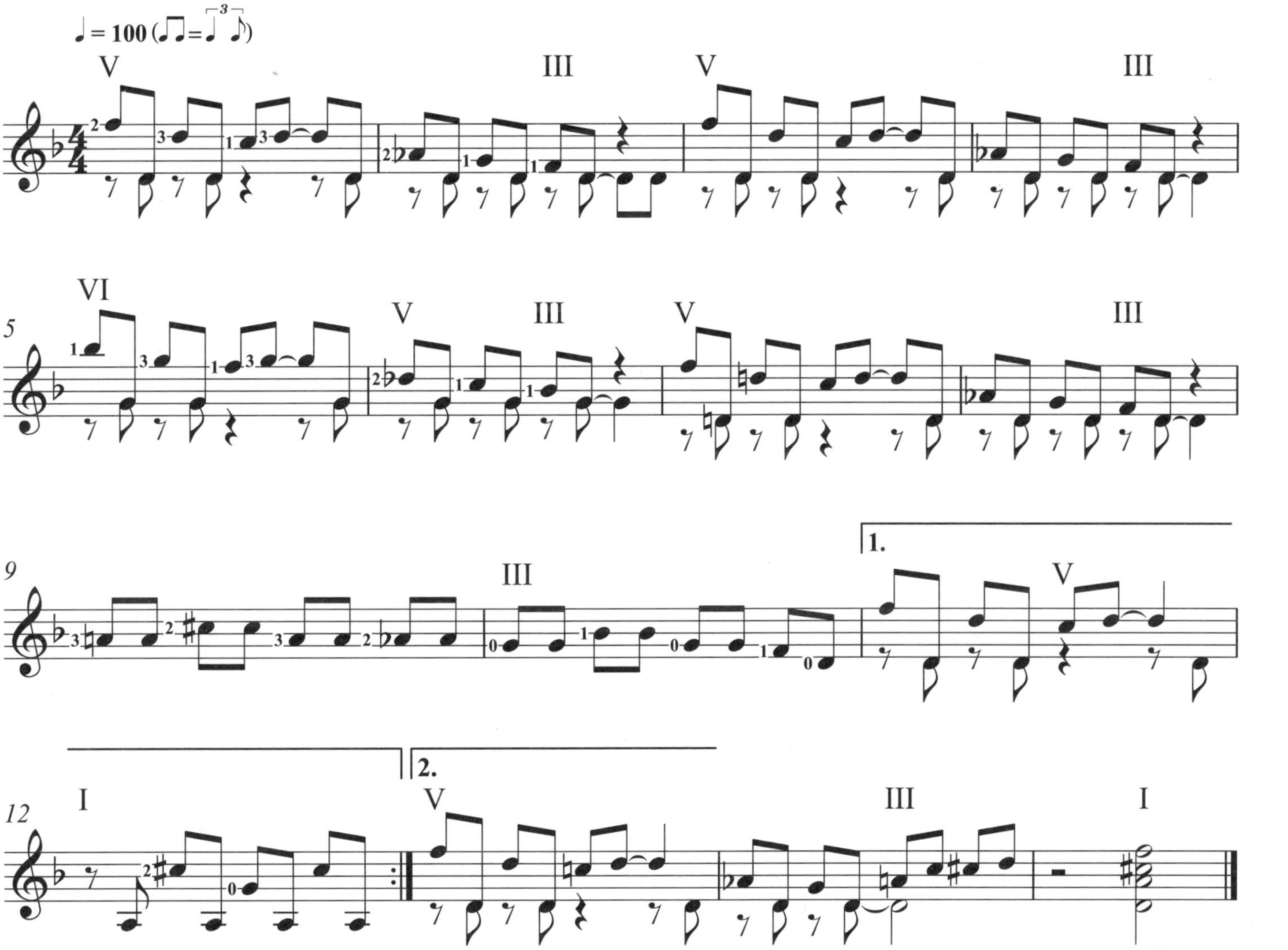

Semiquavers and Triplets

Exercise 1

1　2　3　4　1 + 2 + 3 + 4 +　1　2 + 3　4　1　2 + 3　4 +

Exercise 2

1　+　2　+　1 e + a 2 e + a　1　+ a 2　+　1　a 2　+

Exercise 3

1 2 3 4 5 6　1 2 3 4 5 6　1 2 3 2 2 3　1 2 3 2 2 3

Exercise 4

1　a 2　+　1　a 2　+　1　a 2　+　1　2　3　2　+

Habanera Exercise

Habanera

Greensleeves

Anon.

A Toy Exercise 1

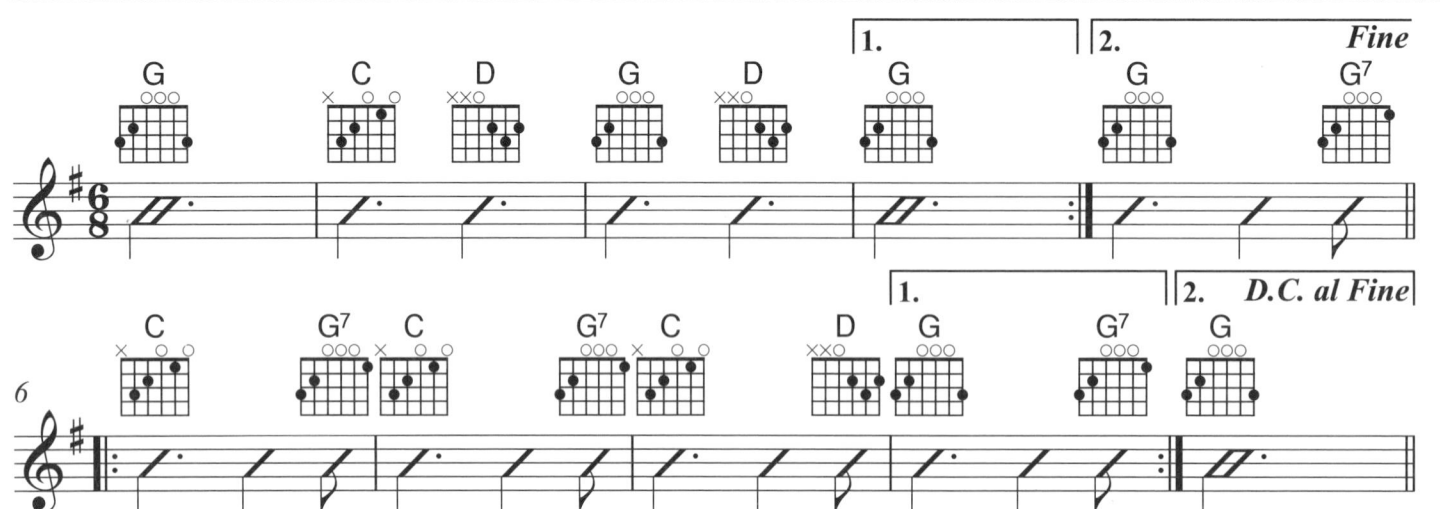

A Toy Exercise 2

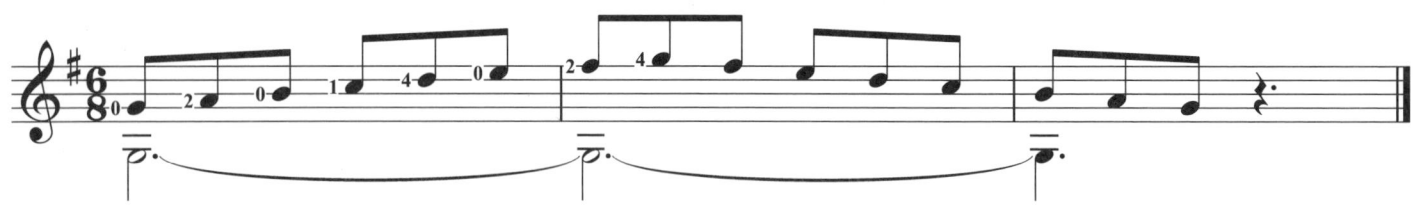

A Toy

Anon.

L.A.